Dedicated to the courage,
love, power and peace within
each one of us.

All ages benefit from sharing
these pages.
Offered without a beginning,
without a middle or end,
they are designed to be of
comfort and to help you
identify, label, then make
choices about feelings.

It's O.K. to be scared of the
things that frighten you.

Fear can warn you when
something is wrong.

It hurts when people
don't keep promises.

Children know.

If you spend a lot of time
pretending that everything is
O.K. when it isn't, it's hard
to be your best.

People don't always tell the truth
even when children know it.

Even when it isn't safe to tell
it out loud, try to know what you
feel inside.

If you worry a lot, try instead
to feel your other feelings.

Feelings are meant to flow,
not stay stuck inside.

When you feel sad, it helps to have someone else understand.

Find someone you can talk to
who makes you feel safe.

You can have two feelings
at the same time.

It can be scary when no one will
listen to what is important to you.

If the first person you try to talk to doesn't understand, or gets embarrassed, or changes the subject, try someone else.

It may be hard to find someone
who really believes you matter,
but you do!

In some families real feelings
are not always accepted.

You are capable
of creating change.

You can change the feeling you
are having even if there's
bad stuff around you.

When you believe your inside
feelings or inside thoughts, you
feel your truth.

If your little voice says, "Stop it!"
                notice . . .
If your little voice says,
"This doesn't seem right!"
                    notice . . .
If your little voice says, "I feel safe."
                    notice . . .

Practice trusting
that little voice.

You have a choice of what to
do with each of your feelings.

Sometimes it's a good idea to
just feel what you feel.

In some families, people know
their real feelings.

Learn to say when it's true,
"I feel happy right now!"

Treasure the feeling you have
when you know you have done
your very best.

It's good to know when you
have done what you could.

It feels good to run fast in the
grass with the wind blowing.

It's a great idea to treat others
the way you like to be treated.

Some people know how to be
proud of good work even if they
are feeling grumpy or hurting.

All people have scary dreams
sometimes.

When you are punished
because someone else is angry,
you are not to blame.

If you see someone hurting another, it's O.K. to say, "Stop it!" That's telling your truth.

You can say, "No!" to yourself
when something feels wrong.

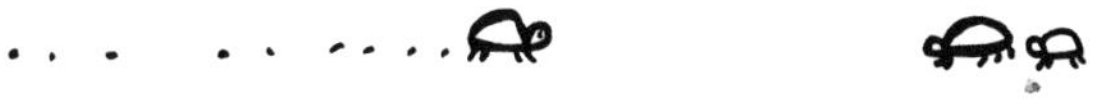

There are many kinds of love.

Having friends feels good.

When you are scared,
it helps to share it.

A warm feeling happens when
you give someone a flower . . .

. . . also when you keep one
for yourself.

In healthy families you can tell
the truth about feelings.

♡ ♡ Good things about ME ♡

1 -
2.
3 -
4 -
5 -
6 -
7 -

♡ ♡ ♡ ♡ ♡ ♡

Make a list of good things
about yourself.

Watching too much TV
can drain your energy.

Learn to take care of yourself.

My list of healthy things

1-

2-

3-

4-

5-

6-

7-

Make a list of healthy
things to do.

Everyone needs to play.

It's good to be with yourself
quietly sometimes.

Be your own cheerleader!

Gratefuls

Purring kitties help; so do sunshine, flowers and support systems such as ours which include family, colleagues and friends, Marshall M. Gelfand, Judy Gelfand and Henry Weiss. Thank you!

We gleaned inspiration from the media wellspring by watching Mr. Rogers on television, listening to David Viscott on the radio and hearing John Bradshaw inter-pret research in useful ways. They do not know us or our work, but we appreciate them, their unique variations on the theme of authenticity and the work they do.

About the Authors

Leslie's intuitive instinct to speak frankly to children in a soft and gentle way guided her back to graduate school for a Master's Degree in Educational Counseling.

Mary's style has evolved from art studies at Syracuse University to her current use of drawings to express her heartfelt reaction to the verbal messages in this book.

Carolyn's first work with children was as a Bilingual/Cross-cultural Specialist in elementary schools. She completed her Doctorate in Psychology and has a private practice in Marin Co., CA.

In some relationships and in some families, it's not that children are told lies, but that they are not told the truth. Prepared with love, these pages are about telling the truth — feeling, knowing and telling the truth.

This book is for all. Parents use it to begin family discussions. Children use it to share their concerns. Counselors use it to open sessions. The whimsical format makes it possible to look at our behavior, be comforted by the truth and reminded that within each one of us is a special resource.

Dear Reader:

If you know a child who is in chaos, where the reality he or she feels and sees is not acknowledged by the adults in charge of his or her life, please be the one to share this book. Other help is available: AA, Al-Anon, Alateen and all Twelve Step programs. Before choosing, interview helping professionals (minister, rabbi, priest, therapist, counselor) to assure their familiarity with family issues and their involvement with Twelve Step programs. A reminder: credentials are helpful, but they are not more important than your own intuition about whom you trust and where you feel safe.

With thankfulness,

Leslie, Mary, Carolyn

"If you keep on doing
what you're doing,
you'll keep on doing it."

Your local bookstore can order it, or we'll help you
order another copy of _Have you ever been a child?_

	Quantity	Total
$ 9.95 each, soft edition CA shipments add $.77 tax per book	_____	$ _____
	....	_____
$ 15.95 each, Deluxe edition CA shipments add $1.24 tax per book	_____	_____
	....	_____
Postage: Add $2.80 -1st book and $2.00 each add'l book	_____	
	Total =	$ _____

___   Check enclosed
___   VISA/MC # and Exp. Date - _____
_____/_____/_____/_____

Signature_____
Daytime phone: (   ) _____
SHIP TO:
Name: _____
Address: _____
City/State/Zip _____

TRINEHEART PUBLISHERS
Dept. B - P.O. Box 600
Palm Springs, CA 92263

For information about quantity discounts, please call
1/800/898-7884

A companion to

HAVE YOU EVER BEEN A CHILD?
(Hints for children and adults)

PRIVATE Keep Out!
(Hints for starting your journal)

is a whimsical, sensitive guide to the art of journalizing for beginners, as well as those more experienced in personal record-keeping. **PRIVATE Keep Out!** will inspire you to more fully experience the richness of your inner life.

Call 1/800-898-7884
to order your copy or a
free catalog.

Your local bookstore can order it, or we'll help you order another copy of _Have you ever been a child?_

	Quantity	Total
$ 9.95 each, soft edition CA shipments add $.77 tax per book	_____	$ _____
	....	_____
$ 15.95 each, Deluxe edition CA shipments add $1.24 tax per book	_____	
	....	_____
Postage: Add $2.80 -1st book and $2.00 each add'l book	_____	
	Total =	$ _____

___   Check enclosed
___   VISA/MC # and Exp. Date - _____
_____/_____/_____/_____

Signature_____
Daytime phone: (   ) _____
SHIP TO:
Name: _____
Address: _____
City/State/Zip _____

 TRINEHEART PUBLISHERS
Dept. B - P.O. Box 600
Palm Springs, CA 92263

For information about quantity discounts, please call
1/800/898-7884

A companion to
HAVE YOU EVER BEEN A CHILD?
(Hints for children and adults)

PRIVATE Keep Out!
(Hints for starting your journal)

is a whimsical, sensitive guide to the art of journalizing for beginners, as well as those more experienced in personal record-keeping. **PRIVATE Keep Out!** will inspire you to more fully experience the richness of your inner life.

Call 1/800-898-7884
to order your copy or a
free catalog.

Your local bookstore can order it, or we'll help you
order another copy of _Have you ever been a child?_

	Quantity	Total
$ 9.95 each, soft edition	_____	$ _____
CA shipments add $.77 tax per book		
....	_____
$ 15.95 each, Deluxe edition	_____	_____
CA shipments add $1.24 tax per book		
....	_____
Postage: Add $2.80 -1st book and $2.00 each add'l book	_____	
	Total =	$ _____

___ Check enclosed
___ VISA/MC # and Exp. Date - _____
_____/_____/_____/_____

Signature_____
Daytime phone: (   ) _____
SHIP TO:
Name: _____
Address: _____
City/State/Zip   _____

 TRINEHEART PUBLISHERS
Dept. B - P.O. Box 600
Palm Springs, CA 92263

For information about quantity discounts, please call
1/800/898-7884

A companion to
HAVE YOU EVER BEEN A CHILD?
(Hints for children and adults)

PRIVATE Keep Out!
(Hints for starting your journal)

is a whimsical, sensitive guide to the art of journalizing for beginners, as well as those more experienced in personal record-keeping. **PRIVATE Keep Out!** will inspire you to more fully experience the richness of your inner life.

Call 1/800-898-7884
to order your copy or a
free catalog.